© Adrian Arbib

Heathcote Williams firmly established himself as one of the most important and inventive writers of our time with his best-selling polemics *Whale Nation*, *Sacred Elephant*, *Falling for a Dolphin* and *Autogeddon*. Many of his works have been adapted for film and television.

A prolific writer, nature enthusiast, political activist and uncompromising observer of the human condition, Williams lives in Oxford.

Badshah Abdul Ghaffar Khan
Islamic Peace Warrior
Frontier Gandhi
And Mountainous Pashtun Giant
Who Defeated a Global Empire
With 'Truth Force' and Guts

An investigative poem by

Heathcote Williams

Acknowledgements

Grateful acknowledgements to the following: Karim Lahham for his scholarship and support; Rajmohan Gandhi; Lutz Kroth; Eddie Mizzi for his assiduous proof-reading; Elena Caldera for her cover design; Martin Wilkinson; Mike Lesser and Claire Palmer of International Times; Oliver Tickell of The Ecologist; Stephen Hunt of Bristol Radical History Workshop; Nigel Allen of Carbon Colour; Dave Motion, Mediatrician, for cybernetic healing; Alan Cox whose video-montage of the poem, produced by Margaret Cox of Handsome Dog Productions, is available online; Joe Allen for his illuminating illustrations; Jacki Klemes for spotting small errors; and lastly to Susan de Muth for her perceptive copy-editing and insightful suggestions. *Sine quibus non.*

"He is a man of penance, also of illumination,
with love for all and hatred towards none."
– Mahatma Gandhi on Ghaffar Khan[1]

First edition Thin Man Press 2015
Copyright © Heathcote Williams
The right of Heathcote Williams to be identified as the Author of the Work has been
asserted by him in accordance with the Copyright, Designs and Patents Act 1988.
All rights reserved. No part of this publication may be reproduced, stored in a retrieval
system, or transmitted, in any form or by any means without the prior written permission of
the publisher.
A CIP catalogue record for this title is available from the British Library
ISBN 978-0-9930141-2-3
Thin Man Press, London
Printed and bound in Great Britain by TJ International Ltd.

Badshah Abdul Ghaffar Khan

Born 6 February 1890

Died 20 January 1988

"The men with guns have become the prayer experts."

– Ghaffar Khan

In the Qur'an's retelling

Of the story of Cain and Abel,

Abel tells his murderous brother,

"If you stretch your hand against me to slay me,

"It is not for me to stretch my hand against you to

slay you;

"For I do fear Allah."[2]

This is the golden text of Islamic nonviolence;

Something that Ghaffar Khan

Urged upon militaristic mullahs,

And upon power-hungry Generals,

And upon those to whom blood feuding

And codes of revenge were endemic.

He'd express the Prophet Muhammad's message

Very simply by saying, "If you plant a slap

After having been provoked by a slap,

Then what is the difference

Between the followers of the Qur'an

And the evildoer?"[3]

To him nonviolence wasn't cowardice

But weaponised goodness.

Another favoured quote was this:

"Fight in the way of Allah those who fight you

"But be not aggressive.

"Surely Allah loves not aggressors."[4]

To Ghaffar Khan the primary meaning of *jihad*

Was not war to spread Islam

But to rescue the weak from persecution.

Ghaffar Khan modestly shrugged off

The profound impact of a revolutionary career,

By saying simply, "I broke useless customs."[5]

Ghaffar Khan preached nonviolence

To a violent culture

And was known as the Gandhi

Of the North-West Frontier Provinces.

"The Holy Prophet Muhammad," said Ghaffar Khan,

"Came into this world and taught us:

"That man is a Muslim

"Who never hurts anyone by word or deed,

"But who works for the benefit and happiness

"Of God's creatures.

"Belief in God is to love one's fellow men."

Ghaffar Khan preached nonviolence

Which, in the Pashto language, he called

Adam tashaddud,

Literally, 'No violence'.

And, improbably, he preached nonviolence successfully

To fiercely volatile audiences in Afghanistan

Where babes-in-arms are brought up with guns.

He preached *sabr*, a renunciation by the strong

Of retaliation; "bowing before the blow

Without a sound or complaint".

And he quoted the mystic Umar, "*Sabr* is revealed

"At the first blow. We have found the best of our life

in *sabr*."

And he quoted al-Gazzali to whom *sabr* was the
        cardinal virtue
In the "'holy war' *(jihad)* between good and evil which
        every human being
"Is called to wage in his or her own heart."

"The law of an eye for an eye," Ghaffar Khan said,
"May be trumped, as it says in the Qur'an,
"By exercising self-restraint
"And by not retaliating.
"Forbearance, forgiveness and self-restraint
"Are acts of atonement;
"A way to share in the tranquillity of Allah."[6]

Ghaffar Khan's son Ghani would say of him,
        "Badshah Khan
"Has discovered that love can create more in a second
"Than bombs can create in a century;
"That the kindest strength is the greatest strength;
"That the only way to be truly brave is to be in the right;
"These are the things he has taught the Pashtun."[7]

Afghanistan's reactionary mullahs once ruled
That "Ghaffar Khan's Pashtun is the language of hell",
To which Ghaffar Khan retorted by enquiring
Where they'd got their information.

He'd invite charges of apostasy
From those he made uncomfortable
But he was courageous enough
Not to care.

"It's all very well," said Gandhi, who was lost in
        admiration
For the gigantic Pashtun, six feet five inches tall;
Straight-backed, even at ninety-eight years old,
Ghaffar Khan bore the semi-saintly honorific, 'Badshah',
Which meant the Shah of Shahs.

"It's all very well," said Gandhi,
"To be a pacifist in a country like India
"Which has a tradition of nonviolence,
"But it's radically different to preach it

"In the country of the Pashtun, in Afghanistan,

"As does my revered colleague and friend,

"So full of compassion and courage,

"Abdul Ghaffar Khan –

"Badshah Khan."

Ghaffar Khan, the son of a farmer,

Was born in Peshawar.

He became guide, guru, and philosopher-king

To thousands upon thousands of Pashtun.

Huge, grizzle-headed,

With piercing dark eyes and dressed

In a long, billowing home-spun shirt.

A pioneering game-changer,

This nonviolent soldier of Islam,

Khan Badshah Ghaffar Khan

Became Afghanistan's

Peacenik King of Kings.

For centuries Ghaffar Khan's country was caught

Between India and Russia

And used as a buffer in the 'Great Game' –

The region's power struggle.

Ghaffar Khan sought independence from both powers
And the means he chose to do so were unique:
"Love can succeed," he'd say, "where bombs have
      failed."[8]

Ghaffar Khan founded history's first pacifist army
To free Afghanistan from the British,
And in response the British tortured him,
Imprisoned him, shackled him
So that his ankles bled
And forced him to sleep on cold cement floors
In rat-infested prison cells.

They made false accusations that he had conducted
Terror campaigns;
That he had cut telegraph wires and railway lines –
And thus they ensured that he'd spend
Over a quarter of his life in jail.

When moved from prison to prison
His neck was ringed with an iron hoop

From which dangled a piece of wood

Bearing his name, prison number and sentence

And the British routinely shot his followers dead.

Yet, having a magnanimous heart,

He forgave his enemies without a thought –

That is, after he'd defeated them.

Ghaffar Khan's fearlessness would come to mean

That the British were more afraid

Of Ghaffar Khan's nonviolence

Than of any violent opposition –

For the fact was that, leading from the heart,

Ghaffar Khan could command many more people

Than if he had been a violent warlord.

Gandhi said of him: "As early as 1920,

"He had come to recognise in nonviolence a weapon,

"The mightiest in the world,

"And his choice was made."[9]

Starting with his own tribe, the Muhammadzai,

And using empathy rather than fear,

Ghaffar Khan persuaded the warring tribes

Of the North West Frontier Provinces

To give up every weapon they possessed.

"You do not kill the soul that God gave sanctity to.

"The Qur'an tells us that killing one person

 "Is like killing all humanity."

Ghaffar Khan directed the tribal peoples

To what he called

"The finest weapon of the Prophet",

Namely "patience and righteousness".

"That such men," commented Gandhi,

"Who would have killed a human being

"With no more thought than they would kill a sheep

"Or a hen should, at the bidding of one man,

"Have laid down their arms

"And accepted nonviolence as the superior weapon

"Sounds almost like a fairy tale."[10]

Ghaffar Khan preached a revolution of the mind –
He believed that nonviolence transforms
And empowers the human personality
And he so captured people's imaginations
That he was able to raise an army of no less
Than 100,000 nonviolent soldiers.

They were known as the *Khudai Khidmatgars*,

The Servants of God

Or, more colloquially, the Red Shirts

As each was dressed in a *Surkh Posh*, a red shirt,

With matching trousers and red turban.

Each knew the meaning of the colour:

It meant they'd exchange their own blood

For freedom and an independent state.

The *Khudai Khidmatgars*

Were made up of Muslims, Hindus, Christians,

Parsees, Sikhs, and Buddhists

And, since Ghaffar Khan saw God

As far-sighted and sophisticated,

And also as nonviolent,

God's red-shirted servants were to be bound

By the divine example.

"An army of unarmed Pashtuns?" He'd ask,

"Who else would be reckless enough to try it?

"What could take more bravado than facing

"An enemy in a righteous cause

"Neither retreating nor retaliating."[11]

Ghaffar Khan also drew inspiration

From the Buddhist *stupas* and monasteries

Which, as a child he'd been told by his father,

"Had housed a peaceful people".

And later he would say, "Look how deep

"Has been the influence of Buddha in these parts.

"We were all Buddhists once."[12]

And he would meditate on the Buddha's injunction:

"Hatred does not cease by hatred;

"Hatred ceases by love.

"This is an unalterable law."

Ghaffar Khan's father Behram,

The Khan of Utmanzai,

Rode until he was ninety and reputedly 'never told a lie'.

Behram was trusted implicitly with the treasures of the
        tribe

And would never dance attendance on any colonial officer

Even though they might hold his fate in their hands.

"He had no feuds," Ghaffar Khan said proudly of his
        father,

"Because he had forgiven all his enemies.

"He knew no revenge."

Behram's scholarly son

Was cast in the same mould.

Early on Ghaffar Khan was accepted as a *mujaddid* –

One who revives or renews the faith –

And in that capacity Ghaffar Khan insisted

That "Islam is peace and brotherhood."

Those Pashtun who wished to join his "Servants of God" movement,

Would take a solemn oath beginning:

"Since God needs no service…

"I promise to serve humanity in the name of God.

"I promise to refrain from violence and from taking revenge.

"I promise to forgive those who oppress me or treat me with cruelty."[13]

Ghaffar Khan told his *Khudai Khidmatgars*,

"You have to be against all tyrants,

"Whoever they may be, whether individuals or nations…

"You will oppose them."[14]

Ghaffar Khan's aim, and that of the *Khudai Khidmatgars*,

Was to gain freedom, as Ghaffar Khan put it,

"From the foreigners who disgraced us".

"The British police have fired bullets,

"Ruined and looted the houses of the people,

"Broken into pieces all the utensils

"Used for drinking tea and eating food.

"That is why children of the Frontier

"When they see an Englishman

"Are apt to exclaim, 'What! Are you still here!'"[15]

Of the place where he grew up,

Near the ancient city of Charsadda

Between the Indus and the Khyber,

Where Alexander the Great had once walked

And which was thought to be the birthplace of Zoroaster,

Ghaffar Khan said, "there is no spot on earth so
          beautiful",

And he resented Afghanistan being presented,

"As a collection of uncivilized, wild tribes."

"I want to create for them," he declared, "a free world,

"Where they can grow in peace, comfort and happiness.

"I want to kiss the earth heaped on the ruins of their
        homes
"Devastated by a brutal people.

"With my own hands I want to wash
"Their bloodstained clothes.
"I want to sweep their lanes and humble mud-huts…
"I want them to stand on their legs with heads erect
"And then I want to throw down this challenge,
"'Show me another decent, gentle
"And cultured race like them.'"[16]

Ghaffar Khan was the greatest promoter of his fellow
        Pashtun,
Of how they could "hurtle down hillsides
"Like falling boulders, not running but bounding," [17]
And of how they could ascend and descend crags,
Dropping down from foothold to foothold.
"No word means more to a Pashtun," Ghaffar Khan
        would say,
"Than 'honour', so I will harness this honour

"And show my people that real honour and freedom

"Lie in the power of nonviolence."

He would draw upon the most penetrating words

Of the Prophet for, like him, Ghaffar Khan believed

That the most successful victories of all

Came through "patience" and "selflessness"

And through "gentle and brave" tactics.

He'd frequently quote Muhammad's words:

"You will recognise the believers

"In their having mercy for one another,

"And in their love for one another,

"And in their kindness towards one another.

"Like the body, when one member of it hurts,

"The entire body hurts."[18]

He'd say, "There is nothing surprising in a Muslim

"Or a Pashtun like me subscribing to nonviolence.

"It is not a new creed.

"It was followed fourteen hundred years ago by the
      Prophet,
"All the time he was in Mecca...
"But we had so far forgotten it that when
      Mahatma Gandhi
"Placed it before us we thought he was sponsoring a
      novel weapon..."[19]

"But listen," Ghaffar Khan would add,
"When the Muslims of Mecca were oppressed
"And helpless and poor like us
"And the infidels of Mecca
"Were resorting to various sorts of tyrannies over them,
"The Muslims came to the Holy Prophet
"And asked him how they would be able to combat
      infidels.

"The Holy Prophet told them that he would show them
"Something that no power on earth
"Would be able to stand against.
"That thing is patience. Together with righteousness."[20]

Each person aspiring to join the *Khudai Khidmatgar*

Was asked to sign a further pledge:

"I call on God as a witness, and solemnly declare on oath

"That I will abide by the following principles:

"With sincerity and faith, I offer my name for the *Khudai*
>   *Khidmatgar*;

"I will sacrifice my wealth, comfort and self in the service
>   of my nation

"And for the liberation of my country.

"I shall help the oppressed against the oppressor.

"I will always abide by the principle of non-violence.

"I will always perform good and noble deeds.

"I promise to devote at least two hours a day to social work.

"All my efforts will be directed to seeking the will of God

"And not towards mere show or becoming an office-holder."

100,000 signed the pledge and were enrolled.[21]

Ghaffar Khan empowered women

Encouraging them to attend the *azad*,

The Afghan schools which he founded

(Though his schools would be demolished by the British

Who reacted badly to the colonised educating themselves).

Ghaffar Khan would say, "If you wish to know

"How civilized a culture is,

"Look at how they treat their women."

And Ghaffar Khan (who founded a girls' school

In Utmanzai, a rare thing in the Muslim North)

Berated his fellow Pashtun

For their treatment of women.

In a speech at Bhaizai he encouraged women

To step out from behind the veil, to defy *purdah*

And to leave the Middle Ages behind:

"My sisters, God makes no distinction between men and
          women.

"You are today oppressed because men

"Have ignored the commands of God and the Prophet.

"In the Holy Qur'an you have an equal share with men.

"If you study history you will see that there are

"Many scholars and poets among women.

"Today we are the followers of custom

"And we oppress you.

"It is a grave mistake we have made in degrading

women..."[22]

Consequently women were recruited into the *Khudai*

Khidmatgar

To teach and to sing marching songs along with men.

"We are the *Khudai Khidmatgar*.

"By death or wealth unmoved.

"*Inquilab Zindabad*.

"Long Live the Revolution."

– Ghaffar Khan's revolution being to use Islam

To supersede the culture of the gun

And not to reinforce it.

***

To extend its power, the British colonial Government

Had passed laws known as the Rowlatt Bills –

Laws whereby any Pashtun could be detained

Without trial and denied a lawyer

For carrying seditious pamphlets –

They could be punished, in other words,

For communicating anything

That urged freedom for a Pashtun state.

The Pashtun had been persecuted by the British

Since the early nineteenth century

Because the Pashtun controlled the Khyber Pass

Which was the gateway to India's wealth.

So any Pashtun who impeded Britain's progress

Was duly characterised by the British commanders

Of Frontier Forces, such as Sir Neville Chamberlain,

As "less than civilized", a "sub-human savage",

"Cruel as a leopard", "a treacherous murderer".

They were "brutes who must be ruled brutally and by
      brutes",
The British declared as they sent out their toughest troops
To carry out a hundred-and-fifty-year-long regime
Of ruthless and unremitting repression,
Backed up by the gun and the gallows.

It suited the British for the Pashtun
To be cutting each others' throats
In tribal conflicts – 'divide and rule' –
For they were then no threat to the British.

But, should they prove a threat,

Then they could be taken onto their rooftops,

Stripped naked and beaten in front of their families,

Humiliated, and even sodomized with tent poles –

A stratagem used by Roman soldiers

To humiliate and break their captives

And routinely used by the British.

On 23 April 1930, Ghaffar Khan gave a speech at
        Utmanzai

In Waziristan, near the Khyber Pass,

In which he urged resistance to British rule

In every aspect, right across the board:

"The strength that Allah has given Pashtuns,"

Said Ghaffar Khan, "Cannot be found in others.

"Others have used this to pit us against each other

"In our own home

"Instead of us using that strength against them.

"Be careful... think... listen. People do not like

"Our coming together in *jirgas*...

"There will be many against your unity and brotherhood...

"Recognize your enemies and friends, your benefit and

loss,

"Promise me you will educate your Pashtuns.

"Islam is peace and brotherhood."

He wished to establish in Afghanistan

A *dar-al-salam*, a home of peace

To which fellow Muslims would make pilgrimage,

And he urged the Pashtun that their condition

Would never improve as long as they believed

In blood for blood:

"Violence," he explained,

"Creates hatred and fear. Nonviolence generates love,

"Makes one bold."[23]

Then his own boldness urged him to say,

"You Pashtuns are not sheep but tigers.

"You have been reared in slavery.

"Don't bleat, roar like a tiger.[24]

"This is your land, but owing to your disunity

"The *firangis* [foreigners] are occupying it.

"Your children die of hunger and thirst

"While their children are enjoying everything they want.

"Islam asks us to side with the weaker party."[25]

For his opposition to British rule

The British were to describe him

As "a most dangerous convict".[26]

And, according to the *Daily Mail*,

He was "the terrible Abdul Ghaffar Khan,

"A jailbird and a relentless enemy of the British."[27]

He was arrested immediately on his leaving the platform,

Whereupon a large group of *Khudai Khidmatgars*

Marched through Peshawar in protest.

They gathered at the Storytellers' Bazaar, Qissa Khwani,

And, in accordance with the pledges they'd made,

Their protest was nonviolent.

Nonetheless, British armoured cars swarmed

Towards them at high speed,
And killed several people instantly.

Anyone calling out '*najat*' – the Pashto for 'freedom' –
Or defiantly shouting '*swaraj*', meaning 'independence',
Was mown down by gunfire.

Yet the crowd remained unprovoked.
Instead of reacting savagely to the savagery
Displayed by the colonial power,
They offered to disperse,
Provided they could tend to the injured
And gather up their dead.

They asked the troops to leave
While they dealt with the catastrophe,
But the British refused
And instead officiously
Urged the demonstrators
To clear the square.
But the protesters remained –

And remained committed to nonviolence
However much provocation they received.

The British then ordered their troops to open fire
Using Maxim machine guns on an unarmed crowd.
Those in the front fell
Only for other Red Shirts to replace them from behind
Following each salvo.

Ghaffar Khan's Red Shirts bared their chests defiantly
And exposed themselves to British bullets.
They stared down the armed troops.

One *Khudai Khidmatgar* received twenty-one bullet wounds
Before falling,
Yet everyone round him stood their ground
And no one panicked.
No one was thrown by this display of imperial might.
Instead, the members of the *Khudai Khidmatgar*
Repeated "God is Great" and clutched the Qur'an
As they went to their deaths.[28]

An eyewitness recorded that, "This state of things
continued
"From 11 till 5 o'clock in the evening.
"Firing was continued for hours after the people had
dispersed,
"In the by-roads, lanes, sub-lanes, balconies and roofs.
"Anybody and everybody was to be shot on sight.
"Such was this terrible day of the 23rd of April —
"A blood-soaked day in the calendar of the Pashtuns —
"A day of wholesale slaughter."[29]

At the end of that day of slaughter
The body count was four hundred dead.
When the number of corpses became too many,
The British government's ambulance cars took them
away.[30]

The Punjabi poet Zafar Ali Khan
Described the Pashtuns' courage:
"They were not afraid of the Angel of Death.
"They faced bullets valiantly with their chests.

"They preferred death to giving up their precious serenity.

"They showed the miracle of their perseverance to the

       entire world."[31]

Towards evening the British

Summoned two platoons

From the Royal *Garhwal* Rifles –

A crack regiment decorated for gallantry

In the First World War –

But to their surprise,

Then to their apprehension,

The native mercenaries refused to fire

On Ghaffar Khan's nonviolent crowd.[32]

To the *Garhwal* riflemen the protestors were *satyagrahis*,

The possessors of 'soul force' or 'truth force' –

Satya meaning "truth" and *agraha* meaning "insistence"

So that *Satyagrahi* were those who insist on truth –

And to harm *satyagrahis* was taboo.

The *Satyagrahi* were firewalled by their nonviolence.

The *Garhwal* riflemen's spokesman told their officers,

"You may blow us from your guns, if you like…"
(He was referring to the mutiny of 1857
When Indians had been shot from cannons as
    punishment),
"But," he added, "we will not shoot our unarmed
    brethren."[33]

The low-minded strategies
Of the British Empire
Were being exposed
By those with a transcendent courage
And, despite the heavy punishments
The British government meted out
(Court-martialling the riflemen
And sentencing sixty-seven Indian soldiers
To transportation, or to life imprisonment),
The writing was on the wall for the British.

The beginning of the colonial power's end
Was written in the Pashtun blood
That was shed in the Story Tellers' Bazaar.

News of the protestors' god-like guts
In the face of a godless repression
Spawned protests over all India
And a chain-reaction galvanized
The all-India freedom movement,
Leading directly to the independence
Of the entire Indian subcontinent.[34]

The history of the British in Afghanistan
With its serial massacres
Was ending – ended by a 'sweet spot'
Of peaceful power shining out like a ruby
In a tortured timeline.

At least eighty-one wars in the nineteenth century
Were caused by the British
Invading other people's countries,
And three of them were in Afghanistan
Into which the British poured thousands of troops.

But colonialism was seen by the Afghans

As a betrayal of the hospitality

Which they'd once been good enough

To offer their British visitors.

In contrast, thanks to British exceptionalism,

Afghans who defended their own country

Against foreign and exploitative invaders

Were regarded by the British as 'insolent'.

Consequently Afghan insurgents were strapped

To cannons and blown to pieces

And rural tribesmen were hanged or gunned down.

The Afghan cities of Ghazni and Dacca and Jalalabad

Were torched if they showed signs of resistance.

Raids from the air were later conducted by the RAF

With BE2C biplanes, Bristol F2Bs,

De Havilland DH9As

And Handley-Page bombers –

All of them flown in from Britain

To strafe Afghan goatherds,

And to pulverize a country

Where the British had once been welcomed

In accordance with the Afghan proverb,

"Honour the guest, O son.

"Even though he be an infidel, open the door",

And in accordance with the civilized rule

By which Afghans live,

Namely the code of *Pashtunwali*,

The *mehman nawazi melmastia*,

In which "a guest is a gift from God,

"To be fed, clothed and their plates kept full" –

Whatever the cost and whatever the risk.

By way of repayment for Afghan hospitality

The Pashtun region was sequestered by the British
     military.

In 1897, the orchards and gardens of the Tirah Valley
     were ransacked,

Pashtun villages were dynamited and crops were burned,

Their wells and their fruit trees were destroyed,
     and their wells poisoned

As the British tried to starve the Pashtun into submission

By conducting a blockade of their whole country.

Outraged, Ghaffar Khan, banished from the Frontier,

Was arrested upon his defiantly returning

And, being brought before the Deputy Commissioner,
     said to him,

"You have occupied our country

"And now want to bar us from entering it."

He was sentenced to what the British judge described

As "rigorous imprisonment"[35] for three years.

"Rigorous" meant torture and sleeping on concrete.

In the 1920s, in revenge for a defeat at Afghan hands,

The British determined to raze Kabul to the ground.

After repeated attacks, the Afghan King,

King Amanullah, spoke out

And berated the British for their air raids on Kabul

During which his own palace was destroyed.

The King reminded the British of how they'd condemned

The German Zeppelin attacks on their own capital city,

And, in a withering letter to their government,

King Amanullah noted acidly,

"It is a matter of great regret that the throwing of bombs

"By Zeppelins on London

"Was denounced as a most savage act;

"And the bombardment of places of worship and sacred
       spots

"Was considered a most abominable operation,

"While now we see with our own eyes that such
       operations

"Are a habit which is prevalent

"Among the 'civilized people' of the West".[36]

But this crass imperial tide would be turned

And all this repression and destruction

Would be brought to a halt

By the actions of an Islamic peacenik

And his impassioned followers –

Each of them more courageous

Than any colonialist armed to the teeth.

And this peace giant, Ghaffar Khan,

Was able to show that the rule of an Empire,

The largest Empire that the world had ever known –

A mercenary Empire that had invaded

Every corner of the world

In four centuries of plunder and piracy –

Could be up-ended in a trice

By the power of a pacifist Muslim

With almost superhuman powers:

The powers that enabled him to live to ninety-eight

Spending his life leaping and bounding

In and out of chains –

British chains and Pakistani chains –

Through his being kept in prison

For over twenty-seven years

Earning him the title

'*Fakhr-e-Afghan*' - 'Pride of the Pashtuns.'

With a devotional prayer from Gandhi

That "the Frontier Pathans may teach the world

"The priceless lesson of nonviolence."[37]

M.J. Akbar, the editor-in-chief of the Indian newspaper

The Asian Age, said of Ghaffar Khan,

"For a man born into a warrior culture,

"To believe he could take on an Empire

"Just by the strength of his beliefs...

"And to actually make his people believe

"The moment you become violent you become a stooge;

"Boy, was that difficult."

Ghaffar Khan would say of his tactics:

"The British considered a nonviolent Pashtun

"More dangerous than a violent Pashtun,

"And that is why, in 1930,

"They inflicted heinous acts

"To goad them to violence. But they failed.[38]"

In addressing crowds Ghaffar Khan

Dispensed with the glib smiles

Of the practised politician.

There were no hollow gestures,

No vainglorious, attention-seeking waves

At those who'd come to hear him speak,

Instead Ghaffar Khan would scold his audiences

For any reactionary lapses

Such as a love of money

Or a lack of brotherhood.[39]

Nonetheless he was adored –

This mould-breaking phenomenon;

This human lodestone of another Islam

Whose mindset led to a seminal moment in history:

A defining moment in exposing war's redundancy.

Gandhi knew of the added strength which Ghaffar Khan

Had bestowed upon his beloved Pashtun.

And he told them, "My faith is that by adopting
     nonviolence
"You will in fact be rendering a lasting service to India
"And to Islam itself. Yours will be the spiritual strength
"With which you can protect not only Islam
"But even other religions."[40]

To the Indian poet Dom Moraes,
Ghaffar Khan was "this tall old wizard,
"This Pashtun chieftain with the Cassandra tone
"With a great gentleness that cloaks him
"Like a crusader's chain mail
"Who conveyed a peaceful
"And utterly truthful aura."[41]

Many of Ghaffar Khan's followers reached ages of
     over one hundred.
Surviving members of the *Khudai Khidmatgars* –
Ghaffar Khan's red-shirted, red-hatted peacenik gang –
Lived to show that a selfless, stress-free pacifism
Could extend your lifespan.

"This tall old wizard,
This Pashtun chieftain with the Cassandra tone"

When the very last members alive
Were visited by Mukulika Banerjee,
She reported how, "They described to me with passion
"What it was like to be swept up
"In the revolutionary anti-British fervour,
"And to follow an utterly charismatic leader,
"And they vividly conveyed the exhilaration
"Of self-sacrifice."[42]

One of them also described how Ghaffar Khan
Could often be seen carrying cricket stumps and a bat:
Ghaffar Khan loved cricket and was good at it
(Though less good at teaching the British fair play).
They prized the lessons he'd taught the Pashtun,
"Because the Pashtuns were previously addicted
"To violence far more than others,
"They have profited by nonviolence much more."[43]
"They learned to exercise the greatest power of the
          Prophet:
"Patience and righteousness.
"No power on earth can stand against it.[44]"

They recalled other confrontations with the British
Where nonviolence mixed with mockery
Of the colonial power had won the day,
And they remembered that Ghaffar Khan
Always ended his speeches by saying,
"*Stre mashe* – may you never grow tired."

One recalled that Gandhi had said
That, in his home state of Gujarat,
The Pashtun had been "bogeymen"
And that "children had turned pale
"At the very mention of their name.
"For a Pashtun to renounce violence
"Stood for much more in the eyes of the world
"Than for a gentle Hindu to do so."

"Even as the rose fills with its fragrance
"All the air around," Gandhi would say,
"When one hundred thousand *Khudai Khidmatgar*
"Become truly nonviolent,
"Their fragrance will permeate the entire length

"And breadth of the country

"And cure the evil of slavery with which we are

       afflicted."[45]

At the height of British repression,

One of the *Khudai Khidmatgar* had confessed

To Ghaffar Khan,

 "To bear this *zulum* (tyranny)

Without retaliation is hard."[46]

But Ghaffar Khan would teach him Gandhi's strategy:

"I have learned through bitter experience,"

Gandhi would say, "that the one supreme lesson

"Is to conserve my anger,

"And as heat conserved is transmuted into energy,

"Even so our anger controlled

"Can be transmuted into a power

"Which can move the world."

And, as a result, when Gandhi travelled

Through the North-West Frontier

Together with Ghaffar Khan
He was impressed by how much
The *Khudai Khidmatgars*
Had "felt within themselves
"An upsurge of soul-force
"As a sequel to their renouncing arms."[47]

They had been transformed
By Ghaffar Khan, so unceasingly fearless
That he'd be arrested at the age of ninety-five
For protesting military rule in Pakistan,
And in his last campaign he'd demand to know
Of both the Pakistani and Indian governments:
"Why are you producing
"Weapons of mass destruction?
"Gandiji worked for nonviolence."[48]

Fifty years after their spiritual victory over the British
The surviving members of the *Khudai Khidmatgars*
Treasured the memory.

One was fond of quoting Rumi,

"When I turned back from the outer battle

"I set my face toward the inner battle.

"We have returned from the lesser *Jihad*

"We are with the Prophet in the greater *Jihad*."[49]

But sadly for Afghanistan

And for the Pashtun,

Another Empire,

Equally cavalier,

Was waiting in the wings –

One prepared to use trickery,

Followed by genocide,

To make the world safe for its hypocrisy.

The New Empire's fall back position

Is an unvarying violence –

The motto of its Marines

Is "Kill 'em all. Let God Sort 'em Out"…

And this aggressive Empire,

With a vengeful violence

Built into its very system,

Would ape the British

By mounting yet more attacks upon Afghanistan;

Each attack sanctioned by its sabre-rattling Presidents,

Approving air attacks, land attacks, and rocket attacks,

For each US President is an obedient slave

To their country's military-industrial complex

For whom any war is a good war

Since it holds the promise

Of a profitable harvest.

The business of America is business

And war is America's biggest business –

The business of an Empire that's diseased by violence

And whose export is a depraved corporate capitalism

That wears the mask of democracy –

The world's crooked policeman

Who sheds blood for money and whose conduct

Is sanctioned by an heretical misreading

Of a pacifist creed, inexplicably adopted as its state

     religion:

"Jesus H. Christ, die you motherfucking raghead"

Being a sample US shibboleth,

Rather than, "God is great."

Or *al-hubb w'al-salam*, Love and Peace.

In the 1970s, as a Cold War ploy,

The United States set about cultivating

Afghanistan's tribal leaders.

It set about arming them

In order to lure Russia into seeing Afghanistan

As a threat to its borders.

Its cynical purpose was to entice Russia

Into invading Afghanistan.

Afghanistan was a country

Where the US oil company Unocal
Wished to build lengthy pipelines,
And it was a country which also held
The promise of great mineral wealth
With its gold and its rubies
And its lithium and its uranium.

If it provoked a Russian invasion
America could then be seen
As leaping nobly to Afghanistan's defence.

This manipulation of Afghani affairs
Was called 'Operation Cyclone' –
Its intention: to release a whirlwind
That would destroy the Soviet Union.

President Carter's Secretary of State,
The anti-Soviet Zbigniew Brzezinski,
Freely admitted that the goal of their programme
Was to "induce a Soviet military intervention."[50]
And indeed, as soon as this had been arranged,

The US President obligingly announced

That, "The Soviet invasion of Afghanistan

"Is the greatest threat to peace since the Second World

   War."[51]

In collusion with Brzezinski, Carter determined

That Afghanistan would serve as the Soviet Union's

   Vietnam,

A ploy that would plunge Russia into its own intractable

   war.

Unashamedly, the warmongering Brzezinski

Spelled it out,

"I wrote to President Carter.

"We now have the opportunity

"Of giving to the USSR its Vietnam war."[52]

The words were destined

To cast an evil spell upon Afghanistan

If not to threaten the whole world itself.

The US Empire would now be doing its best

To bury the spirit of Ghaffar Khan and of Gandhi
And of the *Khudai Khidmatgars*
And with the Empire's uncontrolled aggression
Would undo their enlightened Islam.

In 1992 (rather than exercising its intelligence),
The House Intelligence Committee
Of the US Congress set aside $200 million
To make war in Afghanistan:
$200 million to stir up opposition
To the Soviet presence
By supplying it with sophisticated weapons,
With AK-47s and with rocket launchers
And with Stinger missiles to shoot Russian helicopters
Out of the sky.

Brzezinki was to say that he couldn't care less
About "stirring up a lot of Muslims
"So long as it brought down the Soviet Union."[53]
But his "stirred-up Muslims" would fatefully morph,
And Brzezinski's Empire would find

That it had sown dragon's teeth.

Years later, his stirred-up Muslims would "vow

"To punish the US for every drop of blood."[54]

Concerned about the growing strength

Of an Islamism armed by the US

And fired up by militaristic heresies,

The Prime Minister of Pakistan, Benazir Bhutto,

Would tell the next US President, George H. W. Bush,

Who was continuing Carter's policy,

"You are creating a Frankenstein..."[55]

Her words were prophetic:

The Americans had persuaded the Afghans

That speaking in the language Americans valued most

      highly, namely violence,

Would give them the most credibility.

From elements of the *mujaheddin* came al-Qaeda

And from the far side of al-Qaeda came ISIS...[56]

And Westerners were beheaded in the desert

In revenge for the West's bloodletting

In Muslim countries,

And a fundamentalist Frankenstein's monster

Which the US Empire had created,

Rose up and punched America in the mouth,

Breaking its front teeth on 9/11.

It swatted New York's twin towers,

Two of its economic engine rooms,

And brought them toppling down

With a couple of swipes,

Just as if it had been King Kong.

Of the $400 million dollars which had lit the initial fuse

Of this chain reaction, $200 million had come

     from the US

With its thousand military bases worldwide,

While $200 million dollars had come

From the Saudi Arabian regime,

The US Empire's close ally –

An oil-fired oligarchy of 20,000 plutocratic princelings,

Rich beyond avarice thanks to their peddling petroleum's

Global poison,

A reactionary regime that's fearful of change

And which maintains its power

By beheading and crucifying its poor

In Riyadh's Meera Square

Nicknamed 'Chop Chop' Square.

Photo: Rod Aydelotte

Saudi Arabia buys $45 billion worth of weapons from the
US each year

To reinforce its state, where a woman can be stoned to
death.

A state which is the spawning ground of Wahhabism –

The decadent heresy of a militant Islam –

And which joins forces with the US,

The corporate Empire,

And gun-fetishizing police state which shoots 40,000

Of its own citizens a year ...

They both join forces to crush Afghanistan

And to subject Ghaffar Khan's Pashtun

To genocide.

And then, just as Carter – the Christian fundamentalist

       Simpleton –

Had declared his admiration for a fundamentalist Islam

So did the confused Ronald Reagan.

Reagan assisted even further and, when Gorbachev

       was eager

To pull his troops out of Afghanistan and make peace,

Reagan, perversely, gave the militants even more arms.

Later, more slings and arrows from the Oval Office

Entered Afghanistan thanks to a new US President,

The louche and salacious William J. Clinton,

A sexual predator who delighted in being sexually serviced

Upon his desk in the Oval Office

By his mistress, Monica Lewinsky,

While, somewhat farcically,

She'd break off to read aloud

Walt Whitman's 'Song of Myself'.

Fearful that media accounts

Of his undignified antics

Were making the President a laughing stock,

Clinton made a duplicitous attempt to deflect the scandal

By launching seventy Cruise missiles toward Afghan soil.

In Khost, Clinton's missiles were known as 'Lewinskys'.

Clinton's excuse was that he wished to punish
     the Afghans

For hosting someone of whom the Americans
     disapproved,

Someone who'd helped the Afghans chase out
     the Russians

And who was now a valued guest in Afghanistan –
Someone to whom they'd granted *nanawatai* or sanctuary.

Clinton promptly dropped missiles on their guest's
      encampment in Afghanistan.
And it would be the perverted Clinton's missiles
That provoked 9/11 by way of retaliation.

Later, America's 'Special Envoy', Richard Holbrooke,
Exposed the grotesque nature of his country's venture
Through his choice of metaphor:
"The US victory [over Afghanistan]", he said,
"Will be like pornography – we'll know it when we
      see it."[57]
It was as if this plump servant of the American Imperium
Was licking his lips in anticipation
Of some undisclosed but obscene excitement.

***

Later, President Obama would escalate attacks on
        Afghanistan
By sending 30,000 US troops there followed by drones –
        his robots –
With their thermobaric missiles that work like
        petrol bombs.

Wiping out children and wedding parties became Obama's
        speciality.
Despite Waziristan being flooded, Obama's missiles
        rained down
On its flood plains so that his victims were boiled alive.

The President spread his own brand of 'Apocalypse porn'
By using 'Whiskey Pete', the US military's nickname for
        White Phosphorus,
A novel napalm whose very dust burns flesh off the bone.
His depleted uranium would destroy Ghaffar Khan's
        Afghanistan.
It would corrode its landscape and contaminate its people.
The imperious Obama described the US as the

"Indispensable country"
And said, "I believe in American exceptionalism
With every fibre of my being."[58]

No different from ISIS, President Obama
Has bragged about his use of drones
Saying, sociopathically, "I'm really good at
       killing people."[59]
Every Tuesday, a secret 'kill list' is placed on
       the President's desk
Which the President is required to sign off:
A US government assassination programme.

The programme counts all military age males
In an Afghanistan strike zone as combatants,
Unless there's explicit intelligence
Posthumously proving them innocent.
This is Murder Incorporated, run from the White House.

***

The US dislikes admitting the number of deaths

That it's caused in the longest war in its history.

In 2005 Donald Rumsfeld gave the excuse that

"Death has a tendency to encourage a

depressing view of war".

But its civilian body count, which it abbreviates

to 'Civ Cas',

Runs into thousands, given the thousands of US drone

strikes and US bombings

And incursions by US forces, special and not so special.

While the US defence department diligently documents

The lives of its own military personnel, the lives of others

don't count

And are deserving only of contempt.

US soldiers take 'selfies' of themselves urinating

On the bodies of dead Afghanis;

In the US prison camp, Bagram, in Afghanistan where

torture is routine

A Bosnian Mullah described how US soldiers

Took five people into a tent

Which was crossed by a metal bar at seven feet high.

They tied them all in a line to the bar,

And then sodomised each one in front of the others.[60]

Two thousand one hundred such photographs of Afghan
        captives being abused in US jails

Have recently been suppressed by the administration –

US torture in Afghanistan being thought to be
        'bad for the nation's image'.[61]

In 2009 President Obama received the Nobel Peace Prize

Even as the country over which he presided

Was spending $700 billion on war and destruction
        that same year,

And even while his and George W. Bush's drone attacks

In the North-West Frontier Provinces –

Ghaffar Khan's homeland –

Were creating 3.2 million refugees.

***

Ghaffar Khan wrote in his autobiography,

Zama Zhwand au Jaddo Jehad (My Life and Struggle),

That, "Violence promotes dislike and hatred.

"Anyone can engage in violence

"But only strong people can practice nonviolence

"Because nonviolence needs courage."

Compare this with the sanctified parade

Of Presidential Panjandrums

In White House after White House,

A bloviating and narcissistic clutch

Of serial killers and war criminals all,

With no guiding principles

Save for US hegemony.

Worshipped as celebrities by their gullible acolytes

All are blackmailed by the US weapons industry –

There being a military contractor or subcontractor

In almost every Congressional district –

They're blackmailed because US voters
Will choose war over unemployment.

Morally, by contrast with the devious midgets of the
      Imperium
Ghaffar Khan matched his Afghan mountains in stature.
Despite his opponents' duplicities being nailed
      by Shakespeare
Four hundred years ago, they were still being practised,
And they'd still proclaim, "*Stuffing the ears of men with false
      reports. I speak of peace,*
"*While covert enmity under the smile of safety wounds the world.*"[62]

Ghaffar Khan's worldview was breathtakingly simple:
"I regard nonviolence as love and violence as hate."[63]
But, along with Gandhi's, it was right-minded and
      prophetic.

Ghaffar Khan opposed the hasty partition
Of India by the British upon their granting independence
And, had both he and Gandhi been listened to,
Millions of lives would have been saved.

"We are passing through critical times…"
      Ghaffar Khan declared
In the midst of waves of frenzied sectarian killings,
And he pointed out, tellingly,
"Some people mislead you in the name of Islam.
"What will Islam and the Muslims gain from these riots
"And the slaughter of children, women and the aged?
"These happenings are against the tenets of the Holy
      Qur'an and the sayings of the Prophet.
"The other day an old Sikh pedlar was murdered
      on the road

"In spite of his willingness to embrace Islam.

"Is this done for the sake of Islam?

"I warn the Muslim League brethren that the fire
        they kindle

"Will spread in a wild blaze and consume everything
        in its way.

"The Leaguers fear Hindu domination, while we fear
        British domination.

"Let us meet together and convince each other.

"We can patch up our differences today if we meet
        like brothers."[64]

At the height of the communal riots during partition,

The *Khudai Khidmatgar* stepped forward to protect Hindu
        and Sikh minorities,[65]

But in Ghaffar Khan's concern for a caring Islam and for
        freedom for the Pashtun

He clashed with the military governments of Pakistan.

"I have witnessed the show of the Pakistan Constituent
        Assembly," he said,

"And concluded there is absolutely no difference

"Between the Pakistani leaders

"And the old British bureaucracy."[66]

He regarded Pakistan's politicians with contempt:

"You talk a lot but you don't know how to work.

"It seems as if you think that to clap, give or hear
            speeches is work.

"You beg from other countries but you don't remember
            your poor."[67]

He was promptly jailed for "anti-state activities"[68]

And for "fomenting open sedition";[69]

For these remarks he was jailed for five and a half years

In Montgomery Jail in West Punjab.

"The treatment that was meted out to me in this Islamic

"State of ours was such that I do not even like to mention

"It to you," Ghaffar Khan said, objecting to those who

"Advertized their Islam, and used it for politics

"Rather than for justice or service."[70]

And he would comment on the militarism of a country

Which had declared that Islam was its state religion,
"The men with guns have become the prayer experts"
(*Bandookwale mamaazi ho gaye hain*).[71]

He was locked up for sedition by successive Pakistani
       Presidents –
By General Zia-ul-Haq and by Zulfikar Ali Bhutto–
And, for raising objections to General Zia's
Having granted the Americans facilities
In the North-West Frontier Provinces,
He was arrested at the age of ninety-three,
Charged with subversion
And imprisoned in Khesghi Jail.[72]

Toward the end of his life, Ghaffar Khan,
The Tiger of the Pashtun, was asked
Whether he felt it had all been in vain –
What with periods of military rule in Pakistan,
And what with spiralling violence,
And what with civil war in Afghanistan.
Abdul Ghaffar, 'servant of the all-forgiving',

Looked at the journalist and said quietly,
"I was placed here to plant a seed."

Someone who was present said,
"There was no rancour or bitterness about him,
"In spite of the betrayals and forgetting".
"I was placed here to plant a seed," Ghaffar Khan
      repeated.
"While the British could suppress violence ruthlessly,
"Nonviolence stunned them."

Another Empire has arisen:
An Empire which has waged war
On Muslim country, after Muslim country
After Muslim country...
An Empire determined to provoke violence
And to sow dragon's teeth by its actions.

Alarmist Western Islamophobes warn
Of Muslim barbarians at the gates...
Yet, comparing the self-regarding staccato braying

Of a bullying US mob: "USA! USA! USA!"

And comparing its petty pride at being part

Of the largest Empire in history;

An Empire with the biggest war budgets known to

      mankind

An Empire that's slaughtered thirty million

Since the end of World War Two...[73]

Comparing this with the gentler message from the Qur'an:

"Be not aggressive,"

"Surely Allah loves not aggressors"

There is no comparison.

And there is certainly none

With Ghaffar Khan's seminal message,

"I regard nonviolence as love and violence as hate."

ENDNOTES

[1] Tendulkar, Dinanath Gopal. 1967. *Abdul Ghaffar Khan: Faith is a Battle*: p.437–8. Popular Prakashan (Bombay).

[2] Qur'an 5 (The Table):28

[3] Ramu, P.S. (1969) *Badshah Khan: Indo-Pakistan Relations:* p. 93. S.S. Publishers (Delhi).

[4] Qur'an, 2 (The Cow):190

[5] Haridev Sharma (July 10, 1968). Oral History Transcript, *Interview with Badshah Khan*, Nehru Museum and Memorial Library, New Delhi: p. 15

[6] Qur'an 5 (The Table):45; Qur'an 48 (The Victory):26

[7] Easwaran, Eknath (1999). *Nonviolent Soldier of Islam: Badshah Khan, a Man to Match his Mountains:* p. 101. Nilgiri Press (California).

[8] Tendulkar, *op. cit.* p. 384–386

[9] Tendulkar, *op. cit.* p. 283

[10] Easwaran, *op. cit.* p.20

[11] Easwaran *op. cit.* p. 111

[12] Pyarelal (1966), *Thrown to the Wolves, Abdul Ghaffar* : p.127. Eastlight Book House (Calcutta).

[13] Tendulkar, *op. cit.* p. 59

[14] Easwaran, *op. cit.* p. 199

[15] Tendulkar, *op. cit.* p 186–192

[16] Gandhi, Rajmohan (2004). *Ghaffar Khan: Nonviolent Badshah of the Pakhtuns:* p. 8, Penguin Books (India).

[17] *Ibid* p.13

[18] The Holy Prophet in *Bukhari*.

[19] Tendulkar, *op. cit.* p. 94.

[20] Ramu, P.S. (1992). *Abdul Ghaffar Khan, 1890–1988, Khudai Khidmatgar and National Movement: Momentous Speeches of Badshah Khan*: p.102. SS Publishers (Delhi).

[21] Estimates on the number of members who joined the movement vary widely, Gandhi's secretary, Pyarelal, claims that in the 1930s the number was actually much greater than 100,000.

[22] Easwaran, *op. cit.* p. 133

[23] Puri, G.L (1985). *Khan Abdul Ghaffar Khan: a True Servant of Humanity*: p.xviii. Congress Centenary Celebrations Committee publication (New Delhi).

[24] Tendulkar, *op. cit.* p. 46

[25] Tendulkar, *op. cit.* p. 78

[26] Gandhi, *op. cit.* p. 57

[27] Tendulkar, *op. cit.* p.131

[28] Habibb, Irfan (1997) "Civil Disobedience 1930-31". *Social Scientist* 25 (9–10): pp. 43–66.

[29] Johansen, Robert C. (1997). "Radical Islam and Nonviolence: A Case Study of Religious Empowerment and Constraint Among Pashtuns". *Journal of Peace Research* 34 (1): pp. 53–71.

[30] Khilafat Committee Peshawar (1930), *The Frontier Tragedy*: p.15. Ripon Printing Press (Lahore).

[32] Johansen, *op. cit.* pp. 53–71. A British civil servant wrote later that "hardly any regiment of the Indian Army won greater glory in the Great War

(World War I) than the Garhwal Rifles, and the defection of part of the regiment sent shock waves through India, of apprehension to some, of exultation to others."

[33] Easwaran, *op. cit.* p. 123.

[34] Johansen, *op. cit.* pp. 53–71.

[35] Gandhi, *op. cit.* p. 63.

[36] Singer, Andre (1984). *Lords of the Khyber: The Story of the North-West Frontier:* p.192–193. Faber and Faber (London).

[37] Easwaran, *op. cit.* p. 155.

[38] Tendulkar, *op. cit.* p. 161.

[39] Khan, Abdul Ghaffar (1969). *My Life and Struggle: Autobiography of Badshah Khan (as Narrated to K.B. Narang)*: p.220. Hind Pocket Books (Delhi).

[40] Easwaran, *op. cit* p. 157

[41] Ramu, *op. cit.* p.102

[42] Banerjee, Mukulika (2000). *The Pathan Unarmed: Opposition & Memory in the North West Frontier:* p.7. Oxford University Press (Oxford).

[43] Gandhi, Mahatma. *Collected Works of Mahatma Gandhi*: vol.72, p. 277–78. Publications Division, Ministry of Information & Broadcasting, Government of India.

[44] Easwaran, *op. cit.* p. 117

[45] Easwaran, p. 117

[46] Easwaran, p. 197

[47] Easwaran, p. 198

[48] Easwaran, p. 232

[49] Rumi, Jalal ud-din. *Mathnavi-e-Ma'anavi* I:1386-7

[50] Gibbs, David (2000) "Afghanistan: The Soviet Invasion in Retrospect", *International Politics* 37, no. 2.

[51] Urban, Mark (1988). *War in Afghanistan*: p.56. Macmillan (London).

[52] Kolhatkar, Sonali and Ingalls, James (2006): *Bleeding Afghanistan: Washington, Warlords, and the Propaganda of Silence*: p. 237. Seven Stories Press (New York).

[53] Gibbs, *op. cit.*

[54] http://www.washingtonpost.com/blogs/worldviews/wp/2014/10/16/isl amic-state-fighters-in-new-video-vow-to-punish-u-s-for-every-drop-of-blood/

[55] Hosenball, Mark. "The Road to September 11", *Newsweek* 1 October 2001.

[56] ISIS: Islamic State of Iraq and al-Shams (Syria). The fighting group - which would establish the Islamic State in June 2014 - emerged out of Islamic State of Iraq, an umbrella, jihadist insurgency group, led by al-Qaeda in the Land of the Two Rivers (Iraq).

[57] Tiedemann, Katherine, "Holbrooke on Success", *Foreign Policy*, August 12, 2009.

[58] Obama outlined his foreign policy vision of "might is right" on CNN, May 29, 2014; Transcript of President Obama's interview available in "New Day" programme's archive.

[59] Chumley, Cheryl Kaye in *The Washington Times*, 4 November, 2013.

[60] Deghayes (2007). *The Torture Dossier*, Centre for the Study of Human Rights in the Americas (California)

[61] Ackerman, Spencer. "US ordered to explain withholding of Iraq and Afghanistan torture photos". *Guardian*, 21 October 2014

[62] Shakespeare, William. *Henry IV part 2* Act One Scene 1.

[63] Tendulkar, *op. cit.* p. 465

[64] Tendulkar, p. 419–21

[65] Easwaran, p. 175

[66] Tendulkar, p. 465

[67] Joshi, Haribhau (1970) *Badshah Khan, Kashi: Nagarini Pracharini Sabha*: p. 3

[68] Easwaran, p. 186

[69] Easwaran, p. 185

[70] Gandhi, *op. cit.* p. 253

[71] Gandhi *op. cit.* p. 254

[72] Gandhi, p. 261

[73] Lucas, James A. "Deaths In Other Nations Since WW II Due To US Interventions", 24 April 2007(www.countercurrents.org/lucas240407.htm).

ALSO AVAILABLE FROM THIN MAN PRESS

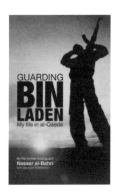

GUARDING BIN LADEN: MY LIFE IN AL-QAEDA

Nasser al-Bahri with Georges Malbrunot

Osama bin Laden's personal bodyguard's memoir. An unrivalled
first-hand account of life in the heart of al-Qaeda as 9/11 was being
plotted. Bahri recounts the jihadists' training and squabbles, his own
stormy relationship with the al-Qaeda boss, and how love for his
wife and young children finally persuaded him to give up his dream
of 'martyrdom' and return to his native Yemen where he was
imprisoned before being personally pardoned by President Saleh.

'Bin Laden's former bodyguard delivers a breath-taking account'
Tele et Vous

'An intriguing glimpse of life inside the al-Qa'ida chief's lair'
Sunday Times

FROM ALBION TO SHANGRI-LA

Peter Doherty (edited by Nina Antonia)

'I will be found a stranger in my own skin. Wonder how I ever let myself in?'. Libertines and Babyshambles frontman, Peter Doherty's latest book, collated from his own diaries and journals, is an intimate chronicle of six tumultuous years as he battles with addiction, the demands of stardom and his hectic love life. Doherty left his notebooks open for friends and fans to scribble in and the book contains poignant entries by Amy Winehouse and Peaches Geldof.

From Albion to Shangri-La has a star rating of 4.8/5 on *Goodreads*

"an engrossing, raw, and at times comically baffling collection of the singer's private diaries dating from 2008 to 2013."

Hollywood Reporter

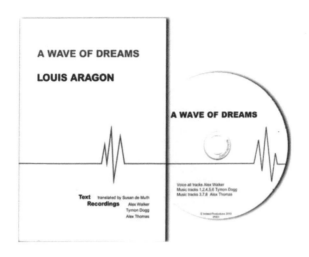

A WAVE OF DREAMS (Book/CD)

Louis Aragon

Louis Aragon's 1924 surrealist prose-poem-essay, is published here
for the first time as a single volume in English. Aragon vividly
describes the inner adventures, the hallucinations and encounters
with the 'Marvelous' which took the young surrealists to the brink of
insanity as a revolutionary new era in Art History was born. The
accompanying CD offers spoken word extracts set in musical
soundscapes by Tymon Dogg & Alex Thomas.

'A leftfield treat...mysteriously opaque and strangely lovely.' Thomas H
Green, Daily Telegraph.

SPARK IN THE DARK

John Constable

The first collection of verse and dramatic prose-poems from *Southwark Mysteries* playwright John Constable. The volume showcases Constable's darkly controversial, high-octane, epic prose-poem, *Wenefer* - a retelling of the Isis and Osiris myth, set in south London's club scene (warning: sex scenes, bad taste and oaths) - as well as political satire and lyrical romances. Constable's 'urban shaman' alter-ego, John Crow, adds strange histories from London's Cross Bones Graveyard where the 'Winchester Geese' (sixteenth century prostitutes licensed by the Bishop of Winchester) are buried.

'Like Shakespeare on Acid' Time Out